SPRING

AS THE EARTH TURNS

Lynn M. Stone

The Rourke Book Co., Inc.
Vero Beach, Florida 32964

Edited by Sandra A. Robinson

PHOTO CREDITS
All photos © Lynn M. Stone

Library of Congress Cataloging-in-Publication Data

Stone, Lynn M.
  Spring / by Lynn M. Stone.
      p. cm. — (As the earth turns)
  Includes index.
  ISBN 1-55916-018-7
  1. Spring—Juvenile literature. [1. Spring.]
I. Title. II. Series: Stone, Lynn M. As the earth turns.
QB637.5.S76 1994
508—dc20   93-41104
                                                     CIP
                                                     AC
Printed in the USA

TABLE OF CONTENTS

SPRING

Spring is a season of new growth after the cold days of winter. Spring brings warmer air and more hours of daylight. Plants begin to grow, and more and more animals become active.

Spring begins on March 20 or 21, depending upon the year. Woodland flowers and other early signs of spring arrive sooner.

A sign of early spring, hepaticas poke through the leafy forest floor

THE SUN AND THE SEASONS

The Earth travels in a year-long path, or **orbit,** around the sun. The tilt of the Earth's poles, or ends, causes the Earth's angle toward the sun to keep changing. Because of that, the amount of sunlight reaching Earth changes slightly each day.

The weather and the seasons change with the amount of sunlight.

The Earth's yearly journey around the sun brings spring and the other three seasons

SPRING NORTH AND SOUTH

The northern **hemisphere,** or half, of the Earth is tilted toward the sun during our spring and summer. Meanwhile, the southern hemisphere is tilting away. That means the southern hemisphere has fall and winter when the northern hemisphere has spring and summer.

Spring begins in September for countries of the southern hemisphere, like Argentina and Australia.

The tilt of the northern half of the world toward the sun loosens the forces of spring

SPRING ARRIVES

Spring arrives with the howl of March winds — but each spring day has more daylight than the one before. Days grow warmer, too. Spring clouds bring more raindrops than snowflakes.

Snowdrifts disappear into puddles. Spring winds blow the puddles dry. Ice crackles, pops and melts away. Winter has lost its bite.

Spring sunlight melts the winter ice around a muskrat's lodge

Springtime in the Arizona desert arrives in March

The nighttime "trill" of toads is springtime music

SPRING FLOWERS

Gentle spring rains and warming soil wake up roots, seeds and trees. First, green sprouts push up through the ground. Soon, blankets of flowers cover the floors of forests and gardens. Then the first leaves on trees begin to grow.

The earliest spring flowers don't wait for winter to disappear. They poke their leaves through the last layer of snow.

The gentle rains of spring turn a woodland green

ANIMALS IN SPRING

New spring plants mean food for animals. Everywhere, creatures are stirring. Some, like the woodchuck and bear, slept winter away in **hibernation.** Spring is a wake-up call!

Snakes crawl out of dens. Frogs and turtles crawl out of pond mud. Toads call for mates. Geese and ducks arrive with the wind, as ice leaves lakes and rivers.

For a woodchuck, spring means repairing a muddy burrow

BABY ANIMALS

Spring is the time when many animals are born. New plants give animals hiding places. Leaves make birds' nests in trees hard to find.

New plants also provide a rich supply of food. Rabbits nibble on fresh grass. Bears gobble salads of new greens.

Many insects hatch in spring. They are food for hungry bats and baby birds.

Just two days old, a gosling — a baby goose — steps into the big, new world

SPRING MEANS …

Spring means pastures to plant, daffodils and tulips to tend.

Spring means the crack of baseball bats, the whistle-calls of cardinals, robins stretching worms.

Spring means trading sleds and skates and snowshoes for bicycles and roller blades.

Spring means drizzle and dampness, sunshine and clover, the rush of wind.

Spring means lots of little birds with big appetites

SPRING AROUND THE WORLD

Spring is not the same all over the world. Let's look at countries near the **equator,** an imaginary line around the Earth's middle.

The middle part of planet Earth doesn't change its angle toward the sun as much as places north and south of the equator do. So all seasons feel like summer near the equator at **sea level.** The changing of seasons near the equator often includes dry or rainy periods.

Glossary

equator (ee KWAY ter) — the imaginary line drawn on maps around the Earth's middle at an equal distance from the north and south poles

hemisphere (HEHM iss fear) — either the northern or southern half of the Earth, using the equator as a divider

hibernation (hi ber NAY shun) — a long, deep winter sleep during which an animal's normal body functions are slowed

orbit (OR bit) — the path that an object follows as it repeatedly travels around another object in space

sea level (SEE LEHV uhl) — the same height, or level, as the sea

INDEX

11/00

GAYLORD S